AF483588

A
Black Male
Treatise on
Contentment

A
Black Male
Treatise on
Contentment

A Journey to Peace Beyond Understanding

Tom Alexander Jr.

ALEXANDER PUBLISHING GROUP, LLC
Dumfries, Virginia

A
Black Male
Treatise on
Contentment

Published by
Alexander Publishing Group, LLC
Dumfries, Virginia
Alexandertom8@gmail.com

Tom Alexander, Jr., Publisher
Yvonne Rose/Quality Press.info, Book Packager

Copyright © 2024 by Tom Alexander Jr., DMin, EdD
ISBN: 979-8-3304-6496-8
Library of Congress Control Number: 2024921251

Dedication

I dedicate this book to all my Black Brothers who have walked through the valley and stood on top of the mountain looking toward an External God whose Shalom (Peace) never leaves nor forsakes us.

A Black Male Treatise on Contentment

Acknowledgements

My journey of contentment would not have been possible without numerous people. I must start with my mother, who has always been a sounding board for me during my most challenging times. She would always let me know that God was with me. Second, my wife Alaisha has been with me through some tough times, and she prayed for me. I also must thank my Aunt Fannie, who is no longer with me, but the memory of her saying "It is going to work out, just keep praying" continues with me. I am grateful for my Aunt Curtisine, Aunt Beatrice, Aunt Helen, and Aunt Sister. Each of them has been there for me. I will not forget Chaplain (COL) Retired Groseclose who introduced me to the book Ordering Your Private World and Pastor Nero, who passed away but his love for me and encouragement is never forgotten. These two men of God provided a source of spiritual strength. I am especially grateful to Lieutenant Colonel retired Sylvaus Johnson, my cousin and mentor, who helped me begin a career in the military, which allowed me to see the world. Then, I must thank my three sons, Jarius, Xavier, and Caleb. Although they are still learning to deal with life's challenges, I have learned so much from their maturity beyond their years. Finally, I acknowledge my father, Tom Alexander Sr. He demonstrated an uncanny resolve to see the world differently than others.

Contents

Preface

Black Male Treatise on Contentment is a devotional focused on the journey of contentment for Black males. Author Tom Alexander Jr. uses Philippians 4 to expand on the different facets of learning to be content. As a husband, father, and a Black man in America, Dr. Alexander guides the reader through this devotional to gain insights and a perspective on the joy of inner peace, which surpasses all understanding. Dr. Alexander shares intimate aspects of his journey to contentment while underpinning the fundamental principles found in Philippians 4. This devotional came into being because Dr. Alexander felt a strong calling to share with his fellow Black brothers, who face the same challenges associated with family, race, and racism in America.

Introduction

I wanted so badly to write a book. I started several versions and stopped. I even wrote a short book after completing my doctorate in divinity. So, what was the difference between wanting and writing? I realized that writing a book is not about putting words on paper; it is about learning to hear and share your inner voice. Psychologists call this inner voice "self-talk." And boy, do I do a lot of self-talk—sometimes to the point that I am exhausted from it.

Self-talk can be positive or negative. Some therapists will tell you to get in touch with your self-talk and listen to see what it tells you. Well, my self-talk often centers around my faith, being a Black man, living in America, being a husband, being a father, a minister, and an educator. Often, my self-talk comes in the morning or late at night when I am no longer distracted from the daily grind of life—things like phone calls, listening to others, watching television, or daydreaming. More often than not, I meditate on a scripture passage. In this book, I've focused on a passage that I often turn to: **Philippians 4.**

PART ONE

PHILIPPIANS 4
THE GROUNDING FORCE

In this book, ***Philippians 4***, is the grounding force for my experience and thoughts as a Black man in America. I share about my upbringing—in the rural south of Mississippi—which has shaped my worldview. I have also had the good fortune of traveling the world, as part of my military experience, to see and be exposed to much more.

Webster defines contentment as a state of happiness. I don't define it in the same manner. Something external must drive the feeling of happiness; if something external must drive the happy feeling, then we can be tossed and driven emotionally by circumstances and situations that may be out of control. Contentment is the ability to center oneself internally, no matter what is occurring externally. Centering is bringing yourself to a place of calm and serenity. I picture Jesus in the midst of the storm at the bottom of the boat, asleep while the boat tossed to and fro. The sky was filled with lightning and thunder. I think of this image when I think of centering.

Another image is one I remember as a little boy on my uncle's ranch. We were all in his cabin, and it had started storming outside. The wind was blowing hard. The rain was coming down. I could see lighting flashing. But during the storm, I saw my uncle's stallion. His head was erect, and he stood sturdy and still. He was calm. I consider the image of Jesus and my Uncle's stallion a potent analogy for understanding contentment. So, as I take you on this journey, I want you to know what I mean by contentment. Especially as Black men, we face storms throughout our lives, and it is crucial to tap into the power of contentment—to be solid and steady with inner peace.

PHILIPPIANS
4:1–20

Therefore, my brothers and sisters, you whom I love and long for, my joy and crown, stand firm in the Lord in this way, dear friends! 2. I plead with Euodia and I plead with Syntyche to be of the same mind in the Lord. 3 Yes, and I ask you, my true companion, help these women since they have contended at my side in the cause of the gospel, along with Clement and the rest of my co-workers, whose names are in the book of life. 4. Rejoice in the Lord always. I will say it again: Rejoice! 5. Let your gentleness be evident to all. The Lord is near. 6. Do not be anxious about anything, but in every situation, by prayer and petition, with thanksgiving, present your requests to God. 7. And the peace of God, which transcends all understanding, will guard your hearts and your minds in Christ Jesus. 8.Finally, brothers and sisters, whatever is true, whatever is noble, whatever is right, whatever is pure, whatever is lovely, whatever is admirable—if anything is excellent or praiseworthy—think about such things. [9] Whatever you have learned or received or heard from me or seen in me—put it into practice. And the God of peace will be with you. [10] I rejoiced greatly in the Lord that at last you renewed your concern for me. Indeed, you were concerned, but you had no opportunity to show it. [11] I am not saying this because I am in need, for I have learned to be content whatever the circumstances. [12] I know what it is to be in need, and I know what it is to have plenty. I have learned the secret of being content in any and every situation, whether well fed or hungry, whether living in plenty or in want. [13] I can do all this through him who gives me strength.[14] Yet it was good of you to share in my troubles. [15] Moreover, as you Philippians know, in the early days of your acquaintance with the gospel, when I set out from Macedonia, not one church shared with me in the matter of giving and receiving, except you only; [16] for even when I was in Thessalonica, you sent me aid more than once when I was in need. [17] Not that I desire your gifts; what I desire is that more be credited to your account. [18] I have received full payment and have more than enough. I am amply supplied, now that I have received from Epaphroditus the gifts you sent. They are a fragrant offering, an acceptable sacrifice, pleasing to God. [19] And my God will meet all your needs according to the riches of his glory in Christ Jesus. [20] To our God and Father be glory for ever and ever. Amen. [21] Greet all God's people in Christ Jesus. The brothers and sisters who are with me send greetings. [22] All God's people here send you greetings, especially those who belong to Caesar's household. [23] The grace of the Lord Jesus Christ be with your spirit. Amen. (New International Version)

HOW TO USE THIS BOOK

A Black Male Treatise on Contentment has 11 sections. Each begins with a selected verse or verses from Philippians. I recommend reading each section as a daily devotional taking time to reflect. Read each section, then use the prayer to further meditate on the concept presented in the particular section. After each section and prayer, there is a personal reflection page. Use it to journal your thoughts on the presented topic. Journaling is a form of gaining insights to your inner thoughts. It has proven to aid in spiritual and emotional well-being.

PART TWO

SELF-TALK TREATISES FOR THE BLACK MAN IN AMERICA

DAY 1

THE WOMEN IN OUR LIVES CAN BE A BIG
SOURCE OF OUR CONTENTMENT

PHILIPPIANS 4:3

Yes, and I ask you, my true companion, help these women since they have contended at my side in the cause of the gospel, along with Clement and the rest of my co-workers, whose names are in the book of life.

Excerpt from "Mother to Son"

So boy, don't you turn back;

Don't you sit down on the steps,

'Cause you finds it's kinder hard;

Don't you fall now—

For I'se still goin,' honey,

I'se still climbin',

And life for me ain't been no crystal stair.

— Langston Hughes

The opening of Philippians has a powerful parallel to my life journey. Much like Paul, a cadre of strong women influenced my life. I am the first grandchild born into a family collective of women who raised me. This family collective was on my maternal side; however, my grandfather passed away before I was born, and I do not have any memories of my grandmother. My mother and father divorced when I was very young, and my mother and I moved back to my mother's hometown, Kone Hill, in Brandon, Mississippi. There, I was influenced by my mother's sister, whom everyone called Fanarien. She was an elementary school teacher and very active in church. Then there were my other aunts: Aunt Bee, Aunt Curt, Aunt Helen, and Aunt Sister. My mother had two brothers: Uncle James and Uncle John, but my aunts influenced me the most. I know many Black men grow up in households run by their mothers or grandmothers. I learned from my experiences very much what the Mother in Mother to Son said to the son.

Life will have obstacles and challenges, but you can't give up; you must keep going.

Black men have long learned perseverance from watching their mothers, grandmothers, and aunts. My mother worked two jobs to ensure I had everything I needed. I witnessed first-hand my Aunt Fannie standing up against injustice in schools to ensure all children got a good education. My other aunts, who were younger, grew up without parents and were able to not only finish high school but also earned a college degree. They set examples for me.

Today, when I hear the misogynistic language in some of our rap music, it hurts my heart. I know it does not allow us as Black men to learn the importance of being gentlemen and show our Black women the respect they deserve. What we fail to understand is that when we denigrate our sisters, we are ultimately destroying ourselves because, as God made clear, "We are all created in God's image." When we don't value our sisters, we are not valuing God, and therefore not valuing ourselves. *So, what is the answer?* It is found again in Philippians. Paul exhorts the reader to uplift and honor Clement and the other women. We must uplift and honor our sisters. We can only find contentment when we value and respect the sisters in our lives.

Dear God,

God, who made it clear that we are all made in Your image. Let us now ask You, God, to forgive us for not honoring and uplifting our sisters. We invite you to create in Us a clean heart and renew in us a spirit of reconciliation. If there is any sister I have wronged, help me seek to regenerate a right relationship with her and you. God, I know that I cannot find real and true contentment without first purging my heart and my mind of any past sin against my sister(s), which will hold me back. I thank all the women in my life who have enabled me to be the brother I am today. Please bless them and provide them the gift of Love they deserve. Thank God, and this I pray. Shalom.

PERSONAL REFLECTION

DAY 2

OUR JOY IS OUR CONTENTMENT

PHILIPPIANS 4:4

Rejoice in the Lord always.
I will say it again: Rejoice!

"This Joy"

This Joy that I have
The world didn't give it to me

....

The world didn't give it
The world can't take it away

— **Shirley Caesar**

There was a hymn sung in my church when I was growing up. The hymn leader, sometimes the preacher, the deacon, or the church mother would start with, "This joy that I have." The entire congregation would then repeat it. The ending of the first part of the hymn was, "the world can't take it away." But so often, we, as Black males, allow the world to steal our joy, not realizing that we are the protectors and owners of it. In Philippians, Paul exhorts us to rejoice.

As an English teacher, I point to the prefix *re*, which means "back or again." This indicates that we start with joy and must return to it as Black men. I believe we are born with a sense of joy. Consider children; if you have watched them, they smile, laugh, and enjoy life. Somehow, as we get older, we drift away from this child-like joy. Black men especially start to encounter challenges in the world. We allow the strains and pull of life to force us to stop smiling as much or even laughing as much. We don't want to show emotion. I have been guilty of this. I wanted to be like Spock, on Star Trek. He never showed emotion and was always logical—but that is not being human.

I have learned that joy does not mean being happy; it means having a strong sense of internal hope. We, as Black men, must tap into our ancestry. So many of those before us who endured slavery were able to survive the harsh and brutal lives and hope for a better future. I want to be clear: I am not simply speaking of a better future after we die; I am speaking of a better future here on earth when we rejoice each day we wake up. When we rejoice that we have life, health, and strength and celebrate how much we have overcome in our lives, we can tap into our ancestry and have unspeakable joy. I no longer seek to be like Spock, because he was not human. I encourage us Black men to rejoice and learn to teach our children and others who we encounter to rejoice as well.

Dear God,

God, who is the center of our joy and the author of our peace. We ask you now to help us return to our place of joy. We ask to embrace daily the sense of hope our ancestors had during the brutal time of slavery. We ask that you forgive us for not believing that we are entitled to laugh and smile. We seek strength to rejoice and model it in a daily walk. God, we thank you for giving us a joy that cannot be taken from us. Amen.

PERSONAL REFLECTION

DAY 3

CONTENTMENT BEGINS WITH ASKING FOR IT

PHILIPPIANS 4:6

Do not be anxious about anything, but in every situation, by prayer and petition, with thanksgiving, present your requests to God.

Jehovah Jirah, Our Provider

I once heard a story about a man who got lost in the middle of the desert. After several days, he had run out of food and water and was afraid that he would die there. Just when he felt it was all over, the man asked God to help him. At that moment, he saw a blur. The blur became a caravan, and he realized he was saved. He said to himself, *God, thank you.*

This story teaches us as Black men that we must know that when we find ourselves in dry and desolate times in our lives, rather than being worried, nervous, and uneasy about the circumstances, we must seek God to help us. Philippians 6 makes it clear that we should not be anxious about anything. It is easier said than done, but practicing asking God to help us by identifying the need in the situation and being thankful in advance creates calmness in any situation. As Black men, we face desert times of feeling that we are lacking or unable to carry on. At the same time, we are often looked upon as the individuals that can withstand anything, so we never ask for help. In asking God to help us, we have to recognize that that may also look like asking our fellow brother or sister to help us.

It is not unmanly to ask for help; it is actually a Godly principle.

So, remember contentment began with asking for it.

Dear God,

Jehovah Jirah, provider, we ask now that you give us a sense of humility to recognize when we need help. God, let us set aside our pride and know that our fellow brothers and sisters are willing to assist us. God, also help us to recognize when to ask others if they need help. We are thankful that you never leave us in a time of need and that you will always supply us with the provisions to help us prosper in this life. Amen.

PERSONAL REFLECTION

DAY 4

PEACE IS CONTENTMENT;
CONTENTMENT IS PEACE

PHILIPPIANS 4:7

And the peace of God, which transcends all understanding, will guard your hearts and your minds in Christ Jesus.

سلام

Salam Alaikum

Philippians 4:7 clarifies that God's peace is incomprehensible to the human mind, but it sets a hedge around our hearts and minds. In Arabic, سلام, *salam alaikum,* is a greeting of "peace be unto you." I share this because it reminds me of my time serving in the military in a combat zone in Iraq. The area was Ramadi. At the time, in 2004, this area was one of the most dangerous places in Iraq because of the improvised explosive devices, grenade attacks, and mortar attacks. My unit's headquarters was in the middle of the desert. Tall concrete barriers fortified the operation base or camp; however, we were always in danger of mortar attacks.

When I first arrived, I found myself unable to sleep because most of the mortar attacks occurred at night. The sound was first a whistle and then a large boom. But I remembered the saying, "Peace be unto you," and I found a calming peace of mind that allowed me to sleep even when I heard the booms. I realized that God was giving me peace beyond my fear of being mortared and a peace that let me know that no matter what, God had me. Even if I die, I will have an external home.

As Black men, we must recognize that God has us, no matter the attacks that come our way—stereotyping, racism, financial attacks. The hardships and even the attacks that may come upon our bodies from sickness. Peace of knowing God has us brings us into a place of contentment. And this kind of peace transcends all.

Dear God,

The God of peace, which surpasses all human understanding, we call upon you. In this very moment, guard our hearts and minds as Black men so we can walk in peace with our brothers and sisters. Remind us, God, that amid a world full of chaos, you are Shalom—peace with us. Thank you now for the peace you have given and will give. Amen.

PERSONAL REFLECTION

DAY 5

CONTENTMENT IS A STATE OF MIND

PHILIPPIANS 4:8

Finally, brothers and sisters, whatever is true, whatever is noble, whatever is right, whatever is pure, whatever is lovely, whatever is admirable— if anything is excellent or praiseworthy—think about such things.

Life's battles don't always go
To the stronger or faster man;
But sooner or later, the person who wins
He is the one who thinks he can!

— **Walter D. Wintle**

I tend to overthink. At least, that's what people have told me. I don't necessarily feel it is a bad trait. It is only bad when I ruminate about past hurt or things out of my control. It is a good thing when I consider the joy of being a husband, a father, a son, a nephew, a cousin, and a friend; and It is a good thing when I remember the first time I went fishing with my mother or the time my father introduced me to a vanilla milkshake. It is a good thing to look back over the hurdles I overcame. As Black men, we have to learn the power of thinking about the good in our lives, because it will bring us joy and contentment.

I'm not naïve to believe that we have not and will not experience trouble and hard times, but the secret to contentment is not dwelling on problems and hard times. We can learn from them, but they should be considered mental weights. Mental weights can make us stronger, not weaker, and we should set them aside and move on in our life.

I love Wintle's line in the poem "Think" because it tells us that our battle to hold on to our joy and peace in this world begins with thinking. Philippians exhorts us to think about the grace given to us by God, God's genuine Love for us, and the marvelous works God has done in our lives. When Black men tap into this state of mind, we lean into the power of contentment.

Dear God,

Bring to my remembrance the joy of my relationship with you and the sweet embrace and comfort you have shown me in times of trouble. Let me not forget that within me is a source of strength that allows me to overcome obstacles, trials, or tribulations. Settle my mind in peace and enshrine my heart in love so that I will walk in the valley of death, fear no evil, and run this race called life with reassurance. Thank you. Amen.

PERSONAL REFLECTION

DAY 6

BEING CONTENT IS A LEARNED BEHAVIOR

PHILIPPIANS 4:9

Whatever you have learned or received or heard from me or seen in me—put it into practice. And the God of peace will be with you.

"Practice does not make perfect.
Only perfect practice makes perfect."

— **Vince Lombardi**

Practicing creates habits; these habits can be good or bad. Doing something wrong over and over again creates a bad habit. Doing something the right way over and over again creates a good habit. In essence, Vince Lombardi's quote says that perfect practice makes perfect. So, when considering Philippians 4:9 and the author's instruction to put into practice what has been learned, received, and heard from the author, the author says, "I have shown you the right way. Practice doing it the right way." Here lies the dilemma for Black men.

We have not always had suitable models or mentors to help us understand what contentment looks and feels like. However, we can start to seek and learn to enshrine it into our very being and way of life. How? Jesus faced constant danger, even from birth, when his family had to travel to Bethlehem. When He did his ministry, crowds would often form, and jealousy and envy of the Pharisees and Scribes would force Him to depart. However, Jesus always focused on His purpose rather than the external circumstances.

As Black men, we can learn from this perfect example of contentment by understanding our purpose. Jesus said that our ultimate purpose is to love God and our neighbor. I will add "love ourselves." We must practice love, which requires patience, long-suffering, perseverance, kindness, and strength. When we practice these things, we practice perfectly and learn to be content. How often have we, as Black men, failed to be patient with others or ourselves? How frequently have we given in or ended up with something we knew was not for our good?

After falling, we find ourselves engrossed in guilt and grief. But if we start to practice love perfectly, we will have contentment. We practice forgiving ourselves and others. Also, practice perfectly seeing others as God sees them and then by treating them as God would. Practice being perfectly strong and humble when faced with difficulties or persecution. We will then begin to feel God's peace, which is contentment.

Dear God,

We come with bowed-down hearts, asking you to teach us the perfect practice of love, which brings about contentment. Give us patience because we know it does not come instantly or overnight, but if we stay steady, it will become a part of who we are. As Black men, we need to be all you have created us to be, so we can be examples. Thank you now for what you will do in advance. Amen.

PERSONAL REFLECTION

DAY 7

OTHERS SUPPORT YOUR CONTENTMENT

PHILIPPIANS 4:10

I rejoiced greatly in the Lord that at last you renewed your concern for me. Indeed, you were concerned, but you had no opportunity to show it.

Excerpt from
"He Ain't Heavy, He's My Brother"

When asked,

"Why weigh yourself down with the load of another?"

I simply smile at them and say,

He ain't heavy, He's my Brother!!

— Bro. Freeman Montague, Jr.

I do not have any biological brothers, but I have so many brothers from another mother: my fraternity brothers of Alpha Phi Alpha, my college brothers, my military brothers, and my church brothers. Within each and every group of brothers, I have found a source of strength in my times of need. The writer of Philippians rejoiced that his companions were concerned for him and finally had an opportunity to check in on him.

As Black men, we sometimes want to treat life like an individual sport—we want to run this race called life alone. Although contentment is personal, it is never compartmentalized as a one-man show. Many of my brothers and sisters have contributed to my regaining my sense of joy because they checked in on me. When they checked in on me, I had to learn to be open to sharing my concerns, not as a way of complaining but as a way of sharing what I was feeling. Sometimes, I would get a straight, "Fix your S$#%." Other times, I would get, "It's okay to feel that way, but don't stay in your feelings." Or sometimes my brother or sister would tell me, "You need to get professional help with this one." Others can support us in our contentment process, and it is okay to give yourself the grace to allow them to do so.

Dear God,

Help me to give myself grace to allow others to help me. Teach me to be okay with saying *Help me,* just as I come openly to you for help. God, as a Black man, open my eyes to see those you have sent as an angel in my life in a time of need. Also, help me to recognize when you want me to put on my wings for another brother or sister. Amen.

PERSONAL REFLECTION

____

____

____

____

____

____

____

____

____

____

____

____

____

____

____

____

____

DAY 8

CONTENTMENT IS NOT CONTINGENT ON ANYTHING ELSE

PHILIPPIANS 4:11–13

(11) I am not saying this because I am in need, for I have learned to be content whatever the circumstances. (12) I know what it is to be in need, and I know what it is to have plenty. I have learned the secret of being content in any and every situation, whether well-fed or hungry, whether living in plenty or in want. (13) I can do all this through him who gives me strength.

"The Strength of My Ancestors"

Though my lashes and bruises are visible

My mind and heart are strong

Though my journey and voyage have been difficult

My faith has not wavered, and my hope lives on

My God Is A Deliverer

So, my Soul Endures All

— **Tom Alexander, Jr.**

The speaker's announcement that being satisfied in whatever state of being is a challenge to us as Black men—living in a world where the pursuit of happiness is often misguided by a desire to have more. To have more money, to be in a higher position, or to have everything be good. True contentment cannot be contingent on anything external, and it cannot be based on a feeling. I authored the poem thinking of our ancestors, who endured the savagery of slavery, the brutality of racism, and the hardships of being Black in America. But so many of them demonstrated a strength of heart and mind and an unwavering faith and hope amid the most hideous conditions.

The speaker in Philippians 4:11–13 makes it clear that in his life, he has had and not had, but he has learned to be content. I am not advocating not striving to achieve goals and desires, but I am advocating that as we strive to achieve our goals and desires, we do not allow whether we achieve our goals and desires to determine whether we are content. When we are in our valley situations, let us be as centered and at peace as we would be in our mountaintop situations. This way of being does not just happen; we learn it and begin to see its power to bring us God's peace.

Dear God,

As Black men, whether we are at a low point in our life or a high point, please help us to learn that your presence is the same so that we can remain at peace. Remind us of how our ancestors traversed the harshness of slavery and racism but also remind us of the victories our brothers and sisters have won. Let us not become complacent, but help us to be content in every situation we find ourselves in. Amen.

PERSONAL REFLECTION

DAY 9

CONTENTMENT DOES NOT MEAN NO TROUBLES

PHILIPPIANS 4:14

Yet it was good of you to share in my troubles.

Excerpt from
"Trouble Don't Last Always,"

May not come when you want Him.

But He's on time

In times of trouble, found Him to be

A friend of mine

In time storm clouds rise

He'll be there.

All your burdens

I know the Lord will help you to bear.

— Rev. Timothy Wright

I hope that, up to this point, you have not thought that learning to be content or being content means a life of smooth sailing. On the contrary, the reason we, as Black men, need to understand and truly learn to be content is that life is hard at times.

Life sometimes comes out like a heavy-weight boxer looking to land that knock-out punch and send you falling on the mat of life. But much like the speaker in Philippians, when we take those punches, we know we are not taking them alone. When I had a severe mental health challenge and it looked like my military career would end; I remember so many people in my life at the time - my mother, aunts, uncles, and friends—reaching out to me, calling me, and sharing in my time of trouble.

There were other times, like when my father was diagnosed with terminal cancer, and at the same time, I was having a serious issue at my job. My mentors and other close associates texted me and called me. Each time, these individuals, during my time of trouble, shared themselves with me to encourage me and sometimes to listen. As Black men, we must realize that we have a community of brothers and sisters who are with us during our troubled times because trouble will come. As others share our troubles to help us through those dark times, we know it will not always last.

Dear God,

We do not ask you to give us a trouble-free life because we know it is not your will. We ask that you help us embrace the storms in our lives. We thank You for knowing that You allow these storms to build our character and enable us to sit with others during their storms. Give us the perseverance and strength to hold to our faith, knowing the storms of life will not last always. Amen.

PERSONAL REFLECTION

DAY 10

CONTENTMENT IS A GIFT YOU GIVE

PHILIPPIANS 4:17

Not that I desire your gifts;

what I desire is that more be credited

to your account.

"Be the change that you wish to see in the world."

— **Mahatma Gandhi**

As we learn to be content, we must recognize that we create an environment of contentment. I have horses, and I have one horse named Buck. One thing about Buck is that he will match your energy. When I ride him, I intentionally stay calm, even when I feel that he is getting anxious.

As Black men, we can be a calming force in our family and community, or we can keep chaos and trouble present. In essence, when we exercise a state of calm, we are giving others around us the gift of contentment. The speaker in Philippians did not desire a gift but desired those he was speaking to, to have it credited to their account. What an excellent concept to become a gift of contentment to those around you facing life's challenges and hardships.

When our brothers and sisters start to seem overwhelmed or in distress, what an incredible gift we can give them of remaining calm and a voice of reason. I imagine a ship's captain standing at the helm of his ship in rocking waters. His crew looks to him as he provides direction and serves as an example of peace. As husbands, fathers, brothers, and friends, we must be that captain giving the gift of contentment to our wives, sons, daughters, brothers, sisters, and friends, even giving it to those who would call themselves our enemies.

Dear God,

Thank you for the gift of contentment. I vow to give it to those around me. Please help me give my contentment to others, especially when life gets hard, and the storms are raging. You have helped me learn to be content, and you have helped me to lead by example. God, I credit the gift to all I encounter. Amen.

PERSONAL REFLECTION

DAY 11

CONTENTMENT IS KNOWING YOU HAVE ALL YOU NEED

PHILIPPIANS 4:19–20

(19) And my God will meet all your needs according to the riches of his glory in Christ Jesus. (20) To our God and Father be glory forever and ever. Amen.

Swahili Proverb

The rich man is not the one who has the most,
but the one who needs the least.

As Black men, sometimes we find ourselves seeking to fill a void with stuff. We pursue becoming a millionaire. We see how many women we can conquer. We look for fame. But in the end, we find no peace. When we learn to be satisfied with what we have before seeking to acquire more, we learn an important lesson about being content. The speaker in Philippians lets us know that God will meet all our needs but notice that it does not say what we want.

One way to gain a sense of contentment is to take inventory of what you really need in life. I must admit that after fifty-plus years, I am now starting to know what I need: such as a close relationship with God and a loving relationship with my wife, sons, and family. I also work daily to leave a positive legacy in my community by giving of myself rather than seeking to get, get, get.

The riches of God's glory are found in loving God and loving others, which is more than enough. This act is contentment. As Black men, let us start looking for ways to give to others rather than simply trying to amass stuff. I am not against economic freedom or educational attainment, but when we make money or gain education, or lose sight of what will last, which is what we do for others, we lose our contentment. Let us be rich in giving to our brothers and sisters by giving of ourselves because we recognize God has given us all we need.

Dear God,

Thank you for meeting my needs, even when I was not appreciative. I now open my heart to know the riches within me and to bless others. I am grateful because you have never left nor forsaken me; when I was in my greatest need, you gave yourself. Let me be the same for my brothers and sisters. Amen.

PERSONAL REFLECTION

Final Word
on Contentment

My final word to you, my brother, is: "know that contentment is a journey, not a destination." Throughout this treatise, I've shared stories from my personal life, and parts of my continued journey of contentment. I share this because we spend so much of our lives thinking that at some point, we will arrive and be at some place. Well, that is a false notion of reality.

Life brings about new challenges and new victories and it is God's plan for us to navigate life to be, rather than to become. The difference between *be* and *become* speaks to the principle of contentment. *Being* is constant, while *becoming* denotes change. Contentment is about a constant connection to the place of joy within, which is the opposite of changing with the wind. Because contentment is a journey, it requires us , as Black men, to be constant and vigilant about holding to our faith. As we travel, and encounter storms or sunny days, we must be steady and constant, because we know that God is the same yesterday, today, and tomorrow.

I pray that your journey of contentment does not stop with reading this book. I pray that I've pointed you along the path of contentment, as the speaker in Philippians presented a peace and joy beyond understanding that will keep your heart and mind.

About the Author

Tom Alexander, Jr. is a mentor, educator, and minister, whose passion and life's work has been to leave a positive legacy in the community, church, and public schools. He completed his doctorate work at Virginia Theological Seminary and The George Washington University.

Dr. Alexander is a husband, father, and son who has experienced many peaks and valleys in his fifty-plus years of living as a Black man in America. He and his wife Alaisha have three sons, Jarius, Xavier, and Caleb.

Dr. Alexander's passion for sharing his journey to contentment comes from watching so many other Black men struggle to find joy and peace in their own lives. ***A Black Male Treatise on Contentment: A Journey to Peace Beyond Understanding*** is Tom Alexander, Jr's first published book.